Guest Book To Celebrate

Thoughts / Messages

Blossom I have missed you so much. We have worked together for the last eighteen years and nothing is the same without you.
I love you so much

NAME: JAcacgueline Walford Brown

Have a beautiful day & Enjoy urself.

Janet

NAME: _____

NAME: June Halstead

4H8 Beach 63rd St #48

Happy Birth To You.
We Love you all the very Best

NAME: _____

Thoughts / Messages

happy birthday To
my One and only
friend blossom
you are the greatest
you are not fake
you are real.
Love Dorret.

NAME: Dorret.

Have a happy
birthday Blossom
I wish you many
more to come. Love
you like an aunt.
from Colleen

NAME:

Love you always.

NAME: Hermine

Happy Birthday

Wishing you all the

best

Ann ntaine + Ms Reid

NAME: Jodie Friends

Thoughts / Messages

Wish you good health love peace happiness. Love Minnie family.
Yvonne Sutherland. Love
~~Jermaine Simpson~~

NAME: Yvonne Sutherland

Collett & Garfield Moran happy Birthday and all the very Best for years to come enjoy it my Dear. Love always

NAME: C Royle Moran

Jermaine Simpson, have a wonderful day and Many happy wishes.

NAME: Jermaine Simpson.

Wishing you a happy Birthday filled with blessings, love and good health.

NAME: Violet Burke

Thoughts / Messages

Oswald Pinnock
Happy Birthday
Blosson

NAME: O Pinnock

Enjoy your birthday
Party food delicious
Music fantastic
God Bless you on your birthday

NAME: Dimples Harris

NAME: Cecile Heath

Happy Birthday May God
help you to live to
See Many more
birthday

NAME:

Thoughts / Messages

TO: My lovely Aunt Blossom ♡ ♡ ♡

First, thank you for all the wonderful food you've cooked for me! Second, thank you for giving me ~~three~~ four beautiful women, I can call my sisters!! I wish you many more Love, Health, & Wealth. God Bless You, I Love You!!

NAME: Lisa (Your 5th & last child)!

TO: Blossom

I love you always. I love the way we raised our children together. We have to work on our second chapter. Our children now have children and we are suppossed to living our golden years having fun. In which we are helping to raise our grandchildren.

NAME: Pat (we'll talk)

Ziggy

NAME: _____

To: the most nicest and most wonderful women I have ever met, I just wanted to wish you a happy birthday and I wish you many more

NAME: Scott

March 30.

Thoughts / Messages

Today is A Bessor
Day.
Dionne First Born.
I Love you muthr

MAS Yourhace

Love Peace

Happyness

NAME: Heath

Dionne Intrisnt
Robinson.

NAME: Faith

Happy

NAME: I love you

NAME:_____

NAME:_____

Thoughts / Messages

NAME:_____

NAME:_____

NAME:_____

NAME:_____

Thoughts / Messages

NAME:_____

NAME:_____

NAME:_____

NAME:_____

Thoughts / Messages

NAME:_____

NAME:_____

NAME:_____

NAME:_____

Thoughts / Messages

NAME:_____

NAME:_____

NAME:_____

NAME:_____

Thoughts / Messages

NAME:_____

NAME:_____

NAME:_____

NAME:_____

Thoughts / Messages

NAME:_____

NAME:_____

NAME:_____

NAME:_____

Thoughts / Messages

NAME:_____

NAME:_____

NAME:_____

NAME:_____

Thoughts / Messages

NAME:_____

NAME:_____

NAME:_____

NAME:_____

Thoughts / Messages

NAME:_____

NAME:_____

NAME:_____

NAME:_____

Thoughts / Messages

NAME:_____

NAME:_____

NAME:_____

NAME:_____

Thoughts / Messages

NAME:_____

NAME:_____

NAME:_____

NAME:_____

Thoughts / Messages

NAME:_____

NAME:_____

NAME:_____

NAME:_____

Thoughts / Messages

NAME:_____

NAME:_____

NAME:_____

NAME:_____

Thoughts / Messages

NAME:_____

NAME:_____

NAME:_____

NAME:_____

Thoughts / Messages

NAME:_____

NAME:_____

NAME:_____

NAME:_____

Thoughts / Messages

NAME:_____

NAME:_____

NAME:_____

NAME:_____

Thoughts / Messages

NAME:_____

NAME:_____

NAME:_____

NAME:_____

Thoughts / Messages

NAME:_____

NAME:_____

NAME:_____

NAME:_____

Thoughts / Messages

NAME:_____

NAME:_____

NAME:_____

NAME:_____

Thoughts / Messages

NAME:_____

NAME:_____

NAME:_____

NAME:_____

Thoughts / Messages

NAME:_____

NAME:_____

NAME:_____

NAME:_____

Thoughts / Messages

NAME:_____

NAME:_____

NAME:_____

NAME:_____

Thoughts / Messages

NAME:_____

NAME:_____

NAME:_____

NAME:_____

Thoughts / Messages

NAME:_____

NAME:_____

NAME:_____

NAME:_____

Thoughts / Messages

NAME:_____

NAME:_____

NAME:_____

NAME:_____

Thoughts / Messages

NAME:_____

NAME:_____

NAME:_____

NAME:_____

Thoughts / Messages

NAME:_____

NAME:_____

NAME:_____

NAME:_____

Thoughts / Messages

NAME:_____

NAME:_____

NAME:_____

NAME:_____

Thoughts / Messages

NAME:_____

NAME:_____

NAME:_____

NAME:_____

Thoughts / Messages

NAME:_____

NAME:_____

NAME:_____

NAME:_____

Thoughts / Messages

NAME:_____

NAME:_____

NAME:_____

NAME:_____

Thoughts / Messages

NAME:_____

NAME:_____

NAME:_____

NAME:_____

Thoughts / Messages

NAME:_____

NAME:_____

NAME:_____

NAME:_____

Thoughts / Messages

NAME:_____

NAME:_____

NAME:_____

NAME:_____

Thoughts / Messages

NAME:_____

NAME:_____

NAME:_____

NAME:_____

Thoughts / Messages

NAME:_____

NAME:_____

NAME:_____

NAME:_____

Thoughts / Messages

NAME:_____

NAME:_____

NAME:_____

NAME:_____

Thoughts / Messages

NAME:_____

NAME:_____

NAME:_____

NAME:_____

Thoughts / Messages

NAME:_____

NAME:_____

NAME:_____

NAME:_____

Thoughts / Messages

NAME:_____

NAME:_____

NAME:_____

NAME:_____

Thoughts / Messages

NAME:_____

NAME:_____

NAME:_____

NAME:_____

Thoughts / Messages

NAME:_____

NAME:_____

NAME:_____

NAME:_____

Thoughts / Messages

NAME:_____

NAME:_____

NAME:_____

NAME:_____

Thoughts / Messages

NAME:_____

NAME:_____

NAME:_____

NAME:_____

Thoughts / Messages

NAME:_____

NAME:_____

NAME:_____

NAME:_____

Thoughts / Messages

NAME:_____

NAME:_____

NAME:_____

NAME:_____

Thoughts / Messages

NAME:_____

NAME:_____

NAME:_____

NAME:_____

Thoughts / Messages

NAME:_____

NAME:_____

NAME:_____

NAME:_____

Thoughts / Messages

NAME:_____

NAME:_____

NAME:_____

NAME:_____

Thoughts / Messages

NAME:_____

NAME:_____

NAME:_____

NAME:_____

Thoughts / Messages

NAME:_____

NAME:_____

NAME:_____

NAME:_____

Thoughts / Messages

NAME:_____

NAME:_____

NAME:_____

NAME:_____

Thoughts / Messages

NAME:_____

NAME:_____

NAME:_____

NAME:_____

Thoughts / Messages

NAME:_____

NAME:_____

NAME:_____

NAME:_____

Thoughts / Messages

NAME:_____

NAME:_____

NAME:_____

NAME:_____

Thoughts / Messages

NAME:_____

NAME:_____

NAME:_____

NAME:_____

Thoughts / Messages

NAME:_____

NAME:_____

NAME:_____

NAME:_____

Thoughts / Messages

NAME:_____

NAME:_____

NAME:_____

NAME:_____

Thoughts / Messages

NAME:_____

NAME:_____

NAME:_____

NAME:_____

Thoughts / Messages

NAME:_____

NAME:_____

NAME:_____

NAME:_____

Thoughts / Messages

NAME:_____

NAME:_____

NAME:_____

NAME:_____

Thoughts / Messages

NAME:_____

NAME:_____

NAME:_____

NAME:_____

Thoughts / Messages

NAME:_____

NAME:_____

NAME:_____

NAME:_____

Thoughts / Messages

NAME:_____

NAME:_____

NAME:_____

NAME:_____

Thoughts / Messages

NAME:_____

NAME:_____

NAME:_____

NAME:_____

Thoughts / Messages

NAME:_____

NAME:_____

NAME:_____

NAME:_____

Thoughts / Messages

NAME:_____

NAME:_____

NAME:_____

NAME:_____

Thoughts / Messages

NAME:_____

NAME:_____

NAME:_____

NAME:_____

Thoughts / Messages

NAME:_____

NAME:_____

NAME:_____

NAME:_____

Thoughts / Messages

NAME:_____

NAME:_____

NAME:_____

NAME:_____

Thoughts / Messages

NAME:_____

NAME:_____

NAME:_____

NAME:_____

Thoughts / Messages

NAME:_____

NAME:_____

NAME:_____

NAME:_____

Thoughts / Messages

NAME:_____

NAME:_____

NAME:_____

NAME:_____

Thoughts / Messages

NAME:_____

NAME:_____

NAME:_____

NAME:_____

Thoughts / Messages

NAME:_____

NAME:_____

NAME:_____

NAME:_____

Thoughts / Messages

NAME:_____

NAME:_____

NAME:_____

NAME:_____

Thoughts / Messages

NAME:_____

NAME:_____

NAME:_____

NAME:_____

Thoughts / Messages

NAME:_____

NAME:_____

NAME:_____

NAME:_____

GIFT LOG

DATE	GIFT DESCRIPTION	GIVEN BY	THANK YOU NOTICE SENT

GIFT LOG

DATE	GIFT DESCRIPTION	GIVEN BY	THANK YOU NOTICE SENT

GIFT LOG

DATE	GIFT DESCRIPTION	GIVEN BY	THANK YOU NOTICE SENT

GIFT LOG

DATE	GIFT DESCRIPTION	GIVEN BY	THANK YOU NOTICE SENT

GIFT LOG

DATE	GIFT DESCRIPTION	GIVEN BY	THANK YOU NOTICE SENT

GIFT LOG

DATE	GIFT DESCRIPTION	GIVEN BY	THANK YOU NOTICE SENT

GIFT LOG

DATE	GIFT DESCRIPTION	GIVEN BY	THANK YOU NOTICE SENT

GIFT LOG

DATE	GIFT DESCRIPTION	GIVEN BY	THANK YOU NOTICE SENT

GIFT LOG

DATE	GIFT DESCRIPTION	GIVEN BY	THANK YOU NOTICE SENT

GIFT LOG

DATE	GIFT DESCRIPTION	GIVEN BY	THANK YOU NOTICE SENT

GIFT LOG

DATE	GIFT DESCRIPTION	GIVEN BY	THANK YOU NOTICE SENT

GIFT LOG

DATE	GIFT DESCRIPTION	GIVEN BY	THANK YOU NOTICE SENT

GIFT LOG

DATE	GIFT DESCRIPTION	GIVEN BY	THANK YOU NOTICE SENT

GIFT LOG

DATE	GIFT DESCRIPTION	GIVEN BY	THANK YOU NOTICE SENT

GIFT LOG

DATE	GIFT DESCRIPTION	GIVEN BY	THANK YOU NOTICE SENT

GIFT LOG

DATE	GIFT DESCRIPTION	GIVEN BY	THANK YOU NOTICE SENT

Made in the USA
Columbia, SC
17 March 2019